LIFESAVING SCIENCE

BODY SCANS

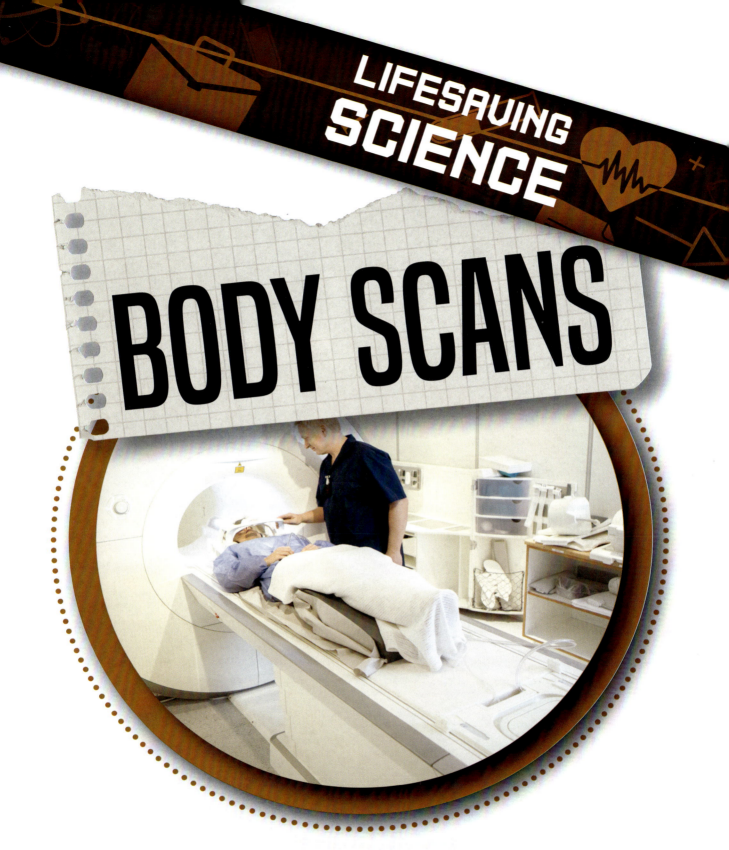

By Joanna Brundle

Published in 2021 by Enslow Publishing, LLC
101 W. 23rd Street, Suite 240,
New York, NY 10011

© 2019 Booklife Publishing
This edition is published by arrangement with Booklife Publishing

All rights reserved.

No part of this book may be reproduced by any means without the written permission of the publisher.

Cataloging-in-Publication Data

Names: Brundle, Joanna.
Title: Body scans / Joanna Brundle.
Description: New York : Enslow Publishing, 2021. | Series: Lifesaving science | Includes glossary and index.
Identifiers: ISBN 9781978519435 (pbk.) | ISBN 9781978519459 (library bound) | ISBN 9781978519442 (6 pack)
Subjects: LCSH: Tomography--Juvenile literature.
Classification: LCC RC78.7.T6 B78 2021 | DDC 616.07'57--dc23

Printed in the United States of America

CPSIA compliance information: Batch #BS20ENS: For further information contact Enslow Publishing, New York, New York at 1-800-542-2595

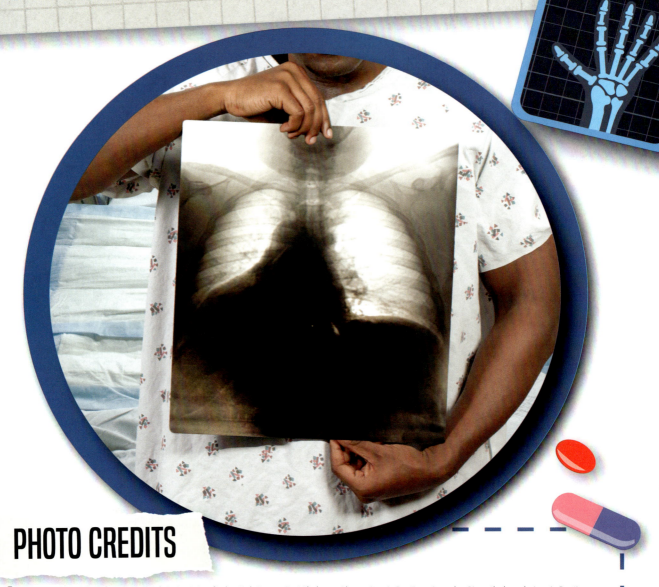

PHOTO CREDITS

Front Cover – Tyler Olson, gst, angkrit. 2 – i viewfinder, Rob Byron. 3 – Nikolayev Alexey, Iconic Bestiary, jagoda, Gigonthebeach, Iconic Bestiary. 4 – Tyler Olson, didesign021. 5 – Romaset, SpeedKingz, OZMedia, peart. 6 – Tyler Olson, PR Image Factory, vertolena. 7 – Tyler Olson, Marcin Balcerzak. 8 – Milagli, svtdesign. 9 – Praisaeng, Africa Studio, create jobs 51. 10 – anatoliy_gleb, Nikolayev Alexey. 11 – Everett Historical, Wilhelm Röntgen. 12 – Suttha Burawonk, Iconic Bestiary. 13 – Tyler Olson. 14 – pang_oasis. 15 – chrisdorney, EmiliaUngur. 16 – Ezz Mika Elya. 17 – LoopAll, Pavel L Photo and Video, Iconic Bestiary. 18 – Sergey Ryzhov, Tyler Olson. 19 – Atthapon Raksthaput, BlueRingMedia, Paramonov Alexander. 20 – faustasyan, Gorodenkoff, jagoda. 21 – whitetherock photo, Alexander Raths. 22 – Designua, Dmytro Zinkevych. 23 – Everett Historical, kalewa. 24 – Ververidis Vasilis, Evellean. 25 – Monet_3k, Juan Aunion. 26 – ballemans. 27 – Monet_3k. 28 – metamorworks, Gigonthebeach. 29 – GaudiLab. 30 – pongmusicstudio, Sarah2. Borders on all pages – Leone_V. Antibiotic vectors throughout – Oxy_gen. Ripped paper throughout – BLACKDAY. Heart rate vector – StudioAz. Logo heart – vector toon. Images are courtesy of Shutterstock.com. With thanks to Getty Images, Thinkstock Photo and iStockphoto.

CONTENTS

PAGE 4	The World of Medicine
PAGE 6	What Are Scans?
PAGE 8	X-Rays
PAGE 12	CT Scans
PAGE 16	MRI Scans
PAGE 20	Ultrasound Scans
PAGE 24	PET Scans
PAGE 28	Scans in the Future
PAGE 30	DEXA Scans
PAGE 31	Glossary
PAGE 32	Index

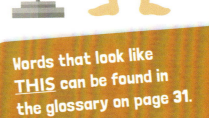

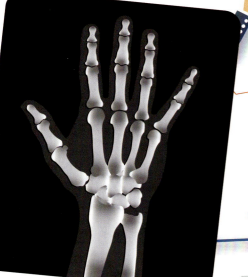

Words that look like **THIS** can be found in the glossary on page 31.

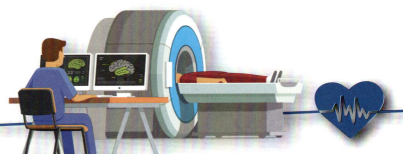

THE WORLD OF MEDICINE

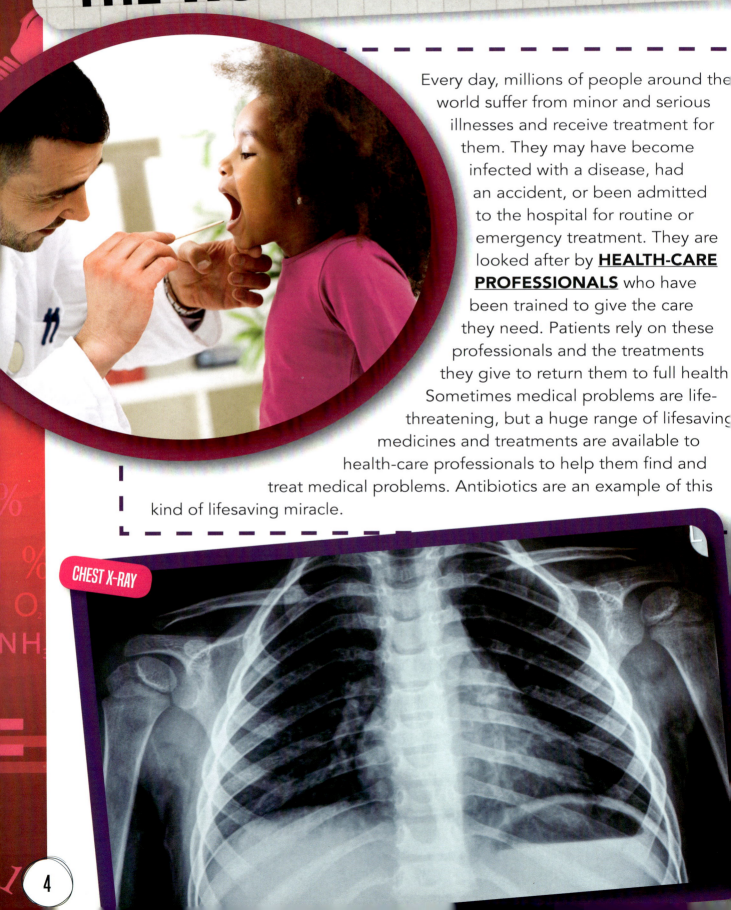

Every day, millions of people around the world suffer from minor and serious illnesses and receive treatment for them. They may have become infected with a disease, had an accident, or been admitted to the hospital for routine or emergency treatment. They are looked after by **HEALTH-CARE PROFESSIONALS** who have been trained to give the care they need. Patients rely on these professionals and the treatments they give to return them to full health. Sometimes medical problems are life-threatening, but a huge range of lifesaving medicines and treatments are available to health-care professionals to help them find and treat medical problems. Antibiotics are an example of this kind of lifesaving miracle.

CHEST X-RAY

Since 1900, worldwide average life expectancy (the amount of time that a newborn baby is expected to live for) has more than doubled and is now over 70 years. Scientists are predicting that average life expectancy will eventually reach over 100 years in some societies. There are many reasons for this. Improved health care has been very important. Scans have played a vital part by enabling doctors to find and treat medical problems quickly and accurately. In many parts of the world, good health and health care are now accepted as normal parts of life, so it is easy to forget that this has not always been the case, and still isn't in some places. Surgery (medical operations) used to be the only way for doctors to see inside a patient's body. Scans now provide clear images, without the need for surgery. In this book, we'll be taking a look at the discovery and development of scans and their lifesaving role in modern medicine.

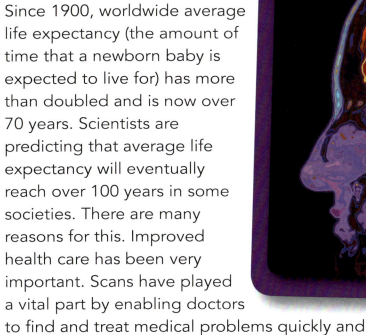

BRAIN SCAN

Scanning equipment can be used to look inside every part of the body.

WHAT ARE SCANS?

Scans are images (pictures) of the inside of the body. They can show solid body tissue, such as bones, and soft body tissue, such as muscles. Scanning is also called imaging or radiology. There are several different types of scans and each one uses particular technology to work. Scans also differ in how accurately each type shows what is happening in different types of body tissue. X-rays, for example, are best for diagnosing broken bones, whereas a type of scan called MRI is best for diagnosing **LIGAMENT** or **CARTILAGE** injuries. Each type of scan also has advantages and disadvantages that must be considered by the doctor before a scan is recommended. An MRI scan, for example, can be a long, noisy process and requires the patient to keep still throughout, so it may not be ideal for children.

Having an X-ray is quick and painless.

FACT

DOCTORS WHO SPECIALIZE IN IMAGING ARE CALLED RADIOLOGISTS.

Airport security scanners also use X-rays to check the contents of passengers' luggage.

WHAT ARE SCANS USED FOR?

Scans can be used to **SCREEN** for possible health problems before a patient has any **SYMPTOMS**. This type of screening can, for example, detect **CANCER** at an early stage, when treatment is much more likely to be effective.

Screening patients for breast cancer (mammography) is estimated to save around one life for every 200 women who are screened.

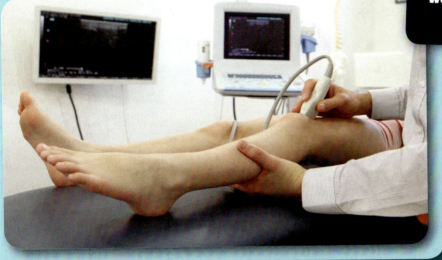

A type of imaging called ultrasound can be used to guide pain-relieving injections in the knee, hip, or shoulder to exactly the right spot.

Doctors also use scans to find out what is causing a patient's symptoms. Scans help them to plan treatment and to check on health conditions that have already been diagnosed. They might, for example, check whether cancer has spread. They can also see if a **TUMOR** is still growing or whether it is shrinking in response to treatment. Surgery is painful, expensive, and requires the patient to spend time recovering, both in the hospital and at home. Scans help a doctor to decide if it is actually needed. They also reduce the need for **EXPLORATORY SURGERY**. When surgery is needed, scans help surgeons to prepare by giving them a clear picture of what to expect inside the patient's body. Doctors also use scans to guide them in taking biopsies accurately. Biopsies involve removing a small piece of tissue that can be studied under a **MICROSCOPE** for signs of disease.

X-RAYS

ELECTROMAGNETIC RADIATION

Electromagnetic radiation is a form of energy that is all around us. The electromagnetic spectrum is the term used by scientists to refer to the entire range of light that exists in the universe. The light that humans can see is called visible light, but most of the light in the universe is not visible to the human eye. Light travels in waves and each type of light in the spectrum has its own wavelength and frequency. X-rays are high-energy light waves that have a short wavelength and a high frequency. They are able to pass through most substances, including body tissue, and thus can be used to form an image of the inside of the body or any other substance being scanned.

THE ELECTROMAGNETIC SPECTRUM

RADIO WAVES · MICROWAVES · INFRARED RADIATION · VISIBLE LIGHT · ULTRAVIOLET RADIATION · X-RAYS · GAMMA RAYS

LIGHT WAVES CHECKLIST

WAVELENGTH
The distance between the **CREST** of one wave and another.

FREQUENCY
The number of crests of a wave that move past a given point in a given amount of time.

HOW DO X-RAYS WORK?

X-rays are the most commonly used type of scan. An X-ray machine looks like a tube containing a big light bulb. It is aimed carefully at the area to be examined and a controlled beam of electromagnetic waves (radiation) is then passed through the patient's body. This radiation cannot be seen by the naked eye and the patient cannot feel anything. Energy from the X-rays is absorbed at different rates by different parts of the body as the X-rays pass through. A detector then picks up the X-rays and converts them into an image. Dense body tissue, such as bones or tumors, absorbs the radiation and appears as white or light areas. Soft tissue, such as the heart and lungs, allows the radiation to pass through. These areas look darker.

This X-ray image shows a break of the patient's left femur (thigh bone).

X-ray images can be viewed on film or as a digital image on a screen.

HAVING AN X-RAY

The part of the patient's body that is to be scanned is placed between the X-ray machine and photographic film or a digital X-ray sensor. The patient must keep still while the image is being taken to ensure the image is clear with no blurring. Several separate X-ray images may be taken at different angles, to give the doctor as much information as possible. X-rays are usually carried out at a hospital in an X-ray department, but they can also be carried out by dentists or other health-care professionals. Sometimes a dye, called a contrast agent, is used to highlight particular areas of the body, such as the kidneys or bladder, so that they can be seen in greater detail. The contrast agent may be swallowed or injected into the patient.

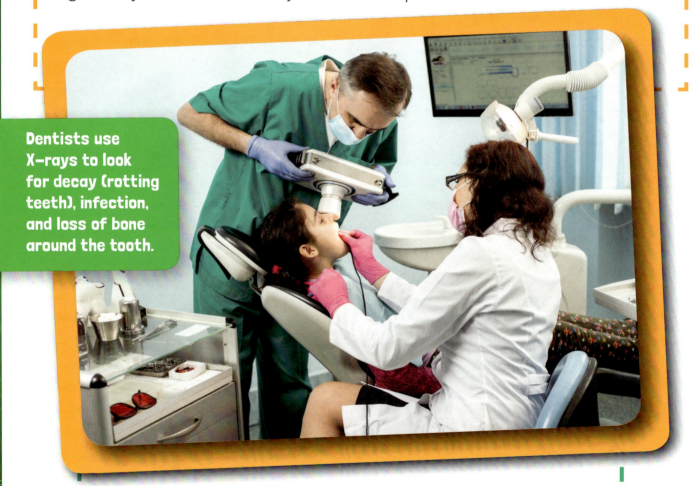

Dentists use X-rays to look for decay (rotting teeth), infection, and loss of bone around the tooth.

The conditions that X-rays can be used to detect include:
- Bone breaks and fractures
- Curving of the spine (scoliosis)
- **CYSTIC FIBROSIS** and other lung conditions
- Swallowing problems (dysphagia)
- Bone tumors
- Breast cancer
- Dental problems such as infection and decay
- Heart conditions

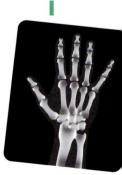

In 1895, a German physicist named Wilhelm Röntgen (1845–1923) was experimenting on a piece of scientific equipment called the Crookes Tube. This was a sealed glass cylinder containing two **ELECTRODES** but no **OXYGEN**. When **HIGH-VOLTAGE** electricity was passed through the tube, the tube gave off a strange glow. A board covered in **PHOSPHORUS** stood just behind Röntgen as he was experimenting. Suddenly, he noticed that it too had started to glow. He used thick, black paper to block the glow from the tube – but the board continued to glow. Röntgen realized that the tube was emitting a previously unknown type of radiation that was passing through the glass. Experiments showed that this radiation could pass through other substances too, including wood and rubber. Röntgen then experimented further, placing his wife Anna Bertha's hand between the activated tube and a **PHOTOGRAPHIC PLATE**. The shadows of her bones and wedding ring were clearly imprinted on the plate. Röntgen had found a way to look inside the body. His discovery was an instant success. Just a month later, doctors were already using X-rays to look at bone fractures.

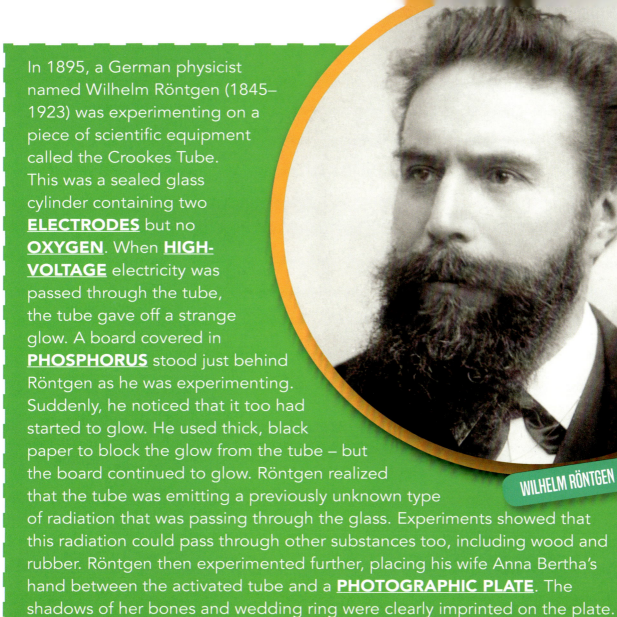

WILHELM RÖNTGEN

In 1901, Röntgen received the **NOBEL PRIZE** for physics for discovering X-rays.

FACT

RÖNTGEN CALLED THE MYSTERIOUS RADIATION HE HAD DISCOVERED X-RAYS BECAUSE, IN MATH, "X" ALWAYS REPRESENTS THE UNKNOWN.

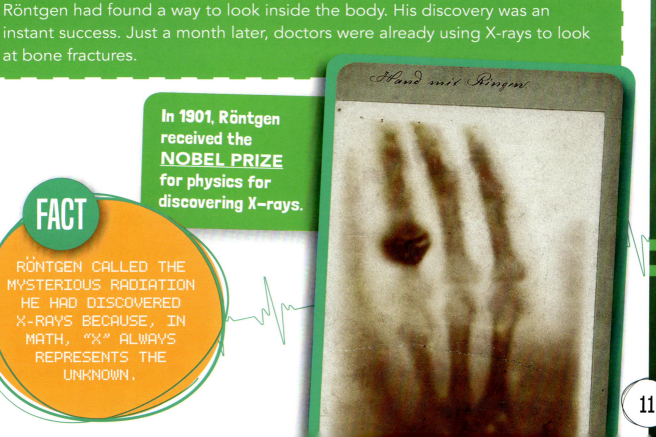

CT SCANS

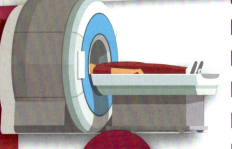

As we've seen, X-rays are a very useful way of seeing inside the body. An X-ray image is, however, only a **TWO-DIMENSIONAL** (2-D) picture of a patient's **THREE-DIMENSIONAL** (3-D) body. There is a limit to what this 2-D image can show. Computerized Tomography (CT) scanning allows a 3-D image of the body to be built up, letting a doctor see inside the body in much greater detail. A CT scan can be used to detect and diagnose a wide range of conditions quickly and accurately. It can show, for example, the size, position, and shape of structures deep within the body, such as the lungs or tumors. In emergency situations, CT scans can show internal damage and bleeding quickly enough for a patient's life to be saved. CT scans are carried out at a hospital by specially trained health-care professionals called radiographers.

FACT

CT SCANS ARE ALSO KNOWN AS CAT (COMPUTERIZED AXIAL TOMOGRAPHY) SCANS.

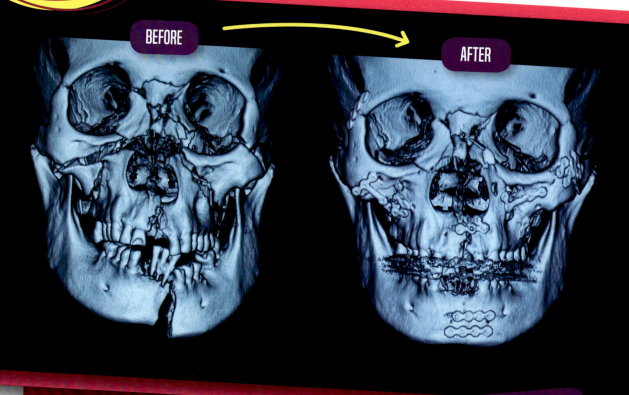

BEFORE → AFTER

CT SCANS OF A CHIN FRACTURE

CT scans can be used before and after treatment to show how well treatment is working.

HOW DO CT SCANS WORK?

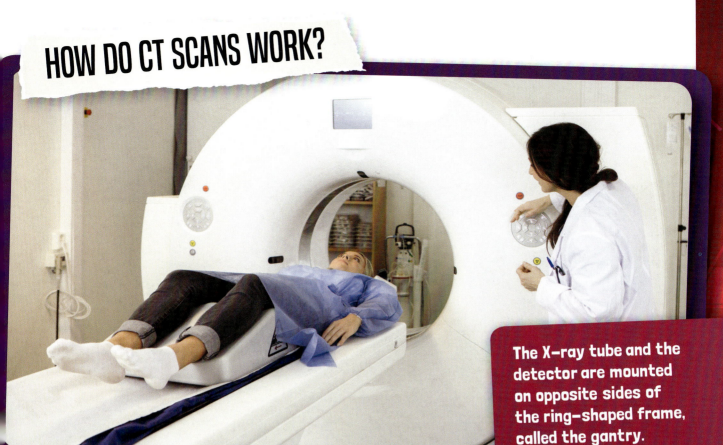

The X-ray tube and the detector are mounted on opposite sides of the ring-shaped frame, called the gantry.

Ordinary X-ray machines emit a single beam of radiation. CT scanners, however, use numerous X-ray beams. A set of electronic X-ray detectors is positioned directly opposite the X-ray source. The scanner, which is the shape of a doughnut, rotates around the patient, delivering the X-ray beams and measuring the amount of radiation that is being absorbed by different parts of the body. The information (data) that the scanner obtains is processed by a computer program. This creates 2-D **CROSS-SECTIONAL** images. Cross-sectional images are called tomographic images. It is useful to think of CT scanning as like looking inside a very thinly sliced loaf of bread. When the image "slices" are put back together by the computer software, a very detailed 3-D image of the inside of the body is visible. As with X-rays, a contrast agent (dye) is sometimes used to highlight a particular area. If images of blood vessels are needed, for example, a contrast agent is injected into the veins.

FACT

SPIRAL CT, ALSO CALLED HELICAL CT, IS A TYPE OF SCANNING IN WHICH THE X-RAY BEAM FROM THE SCANNER MOVES IN A SPIRAL PATH, GATHERING CONTINUOUS DATA, WITH NO GAPS BETWEEN THE IMAGES.

HAVING A CT SCAN

Before the scan, the patient puts on a hospital robe. Anything made of metal, such as jewelry, must be removed because metal interferes with the sensitive equipment. During the scan, the patient lies on their back on a flat bed. The bed moves into the scanner, which then rotates around the section of the body to be scanned as the patient passes through it. A CT scan is painless, but if clear images are to be obtained, the patient must keep still. It is normal to hear a whirring or buzzing noise. The radiographer operates the scanner from the next room.

FACT

MODERN CT SCANNERS ARE SO FAST THAT THEY CAN SCAN THROUGH LARGE SECTIONS OF THE BODY IN JUST A FEW SECONDS. THIS IS HELPFUL IN SCANNING PATIENTS WHO FIND IT HARD TO KEEP STILL, SUCH AS VERY YOUNG CHILDREN.

The radiographer can see, hear, and speak to the patient from the CT control room, using a built-in intercom system.

Examples of the uses of CT scans include:
- Identifying damage to internal **ORGANS** in accident victims
- Detecting, measuring, and locating cancers, especially in the chest, abdomen, and pelvis
- Detecting diseases that can lead to stroke (an interruption of blood flow to the brain) or kidney failure
- Assessing problems affecting children, such as cystic fibrosis
- Planning and looking at the results of organ transplants, cancer treatments, and other procedures
- Assessing patients who are having difficulty breathing

THE DEVELOPMENT OF CT SCANS

The CT scanner was invented by Godfrey Hounsfield (1919–2004), an English electrical engineer who worked for a company called EMI. Hounsfield came up with the idea of combining X-rays and computer technology in 1967. After **RESEARCH** and development, the first CT scanner was installed in a hospital in London in 1971. It was designed only to take pictures of the brain and was originally called the EMI scanner. In 1975, the first whole-body scanner was built. In recognition of his valuable work, Hounsfield was awarded a Nobel Prize in 1979, sharing it with scientist Allan McLeod Cormack (1924–1998).

EMI owned the music of the pop group, the Beatles, and is rumored to have used money made from sales of their records to pay for Hounsfield's work.

FACT

THE SCALE OF MEASUREMENT USED ON ALL CT SCANNERS IS CALLED THE HOUNSFIELD SCALE, AFTER GODFREY HOUNSFIELD.

EFFECTS OF RADIATION

Both X-ray imaging and CT scanning expose the body to a very small amount of radiation. In higher amounts, radiation may slightly increase the risk of a person developing cancer in later life. The risk from scanning is, however, very small compared to the benefits. CT scanning is not usually carried out on pregnant women because of a small risk of damage to the developing baby.

MRI SCANS

Magnetic resonance imaging (MRI) is a type of scan that uses **RADIO WAVES** (see the diagram on page 8) and powerful **MAGNETIC FIELDS** to produce detailed pictures of the inside of a patient's body. Unlike X-rays and CT scans, MRI scans do not use any radiation to produce the images. For this reason, they are often seen as a better choice for children than X-rays or CT scans. MRI scans can be used to look at almost any part of the body. They provide detailed images that help doctors to diagnose and plan treatment for many conditions. MRI scans are painless and cause no known damage. An MRI scan is carried out by a radiographer.

MRI SCANNER

The patient enters the scanner here either head or feet first, depending on the area to be scanned.

MRI scans can be used to:
- Examine bones and joints, the heart and blood vessels, and internal organs such as the brain and liver
- Diagnose problems such as strokes, cancer, and injuries to the back and spine
- Diagnose **MULTIPLE SCLEROSIS** and eye and inner ear problems
- Examine injuries to ligaments and cartilage

HOW DO MRI SCANS WORK?

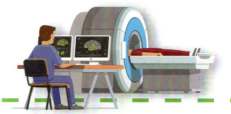

The average human body is made up of around 60% water, most of which is contained inside body **CELLS**. Each water **MOLECULE** is made up of two parts **HYDROGEN** and one part oxygen. In the middle of each hydrogen **ATOM** is a tiny particle called a proton. Protons are like tiny magnets. The powerful magnetic field produced by the scanner has the effect of lining up the hydrogen protons in the same direction. The scanner also produces short bursts of radio waves, which are directed at the body. These waves knock the protons out of alignment. After the radio waves are turned off, the protons return to normal. This process, called precession, produces a radio signal. Receivers in the scanner measure the signal and produce an image. Protons in different body tissues return to normal at different rates and produce different signals. These differences enable the scanner to distinguish between different types of tissue.

ILLUSTRATION OF A WATER MOLECULE

Water H_2O

OXYGEN ATOM

HYDROGEN ATOM

The radiographer controls the scanner using a computer that is housed in a separate control room to protect it from the magnetic field.

FACT

THE MAGNETIC FIELD CREATED BY AN MRI SCANNER IS ABOUT 1,000 TIMES STRONGER THAN A TYPICAL FRIDGE MAGNET!

HAVING AN MRI SCAN

As the scanner produces strong magnetic fields, the patient must first remove any metal objects, such as jewelry. The patient lies on a movable table that slides in and out of the ring-shaped entrance to the scanner. The scanner itself is a tunnel-like tube, open at both ends. The patient can talk to the radiographer during the scan, using an intercom. The diameter of the tube is only about 28 inches (70 cm), so some patients feel **CLAUSTROPHOBIC**. A sedative can be given to these patients to help them relax. Although the scan is painless, it is noisy, with loud tapping and thumping noises as the electric current in the scanner coils is switched on and off. MRI scans can take up to 90 minutes and the patient must keep still to ensure the images are clear. Patients who cannot keep still, such as babies, may be given a **GENERAL ANESTHETIC**. MRI scans are not suitable for patients with metal objects, such as **PACEMAKERS**, inside their bodies.

MRI patients may be given earphones that play music to block out the noise of the scanner.

FACT

NEWER SCANNERS ARE OPEN AT THE SIDES, WHICH HELPS CLAUSTROPHOBIC PATIENTS. SOME ALLOW THE PATIENT TO STAND, WHICH IS USEFUL FOR LOOKING AT HOW JOINTS REACT TO BEARING THE PATIENT'S WEIGHT.

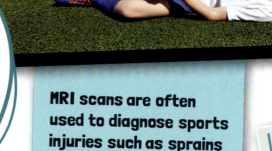

MRI scans are often used to diagnose sports injuries such as sprains and muscle tears.

DIFFUSION MRI, FUNCTIONAL MRI, AND MRA

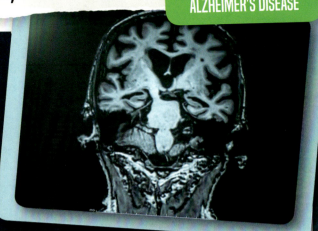

MRI BRAIN SCAN SHOWING ALZHEIMER'S DISEASE

Diffusion MRI scans measure how water diffuses (spreads) through the body. This type of MRI is used to diagnose conditions, such as strokes and tumors, that interfere with this diffusion. Functional MRI (fMRI) measures blood flow to different areas of the brain to check brain activity. This type of MRI is used to diagnose **ALZHEIMER'S DISEASE** and to plan delicate brain surgery. Magnetic resonance angiography (MRA) produces images of flowing blood in almost any part of the body.

HEALTHY BRAIN

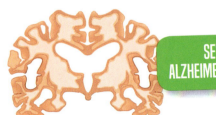

SEVERE ALZHEIMER'S DISEASE

THE DEVELOPMENT OF MRI SCANS

In 1971, American doctor Raymond Damadian (1936–) discovered that magnetic resonance could be used for diagnosing disease when he realized that cancer tumors gave off different signals than healthy tissue. In 1973, American chemist Paul Lauterbur (1929–2007) showed that magnetic resonance could be used to produce images. British scientist Peter Mansfield (1933–2017) then developed mathematical methods for analyzing information in the signal to produce images quickly and accurately. By 1977, Damadian had built the first whole-body scanner, which he named Indomitable.

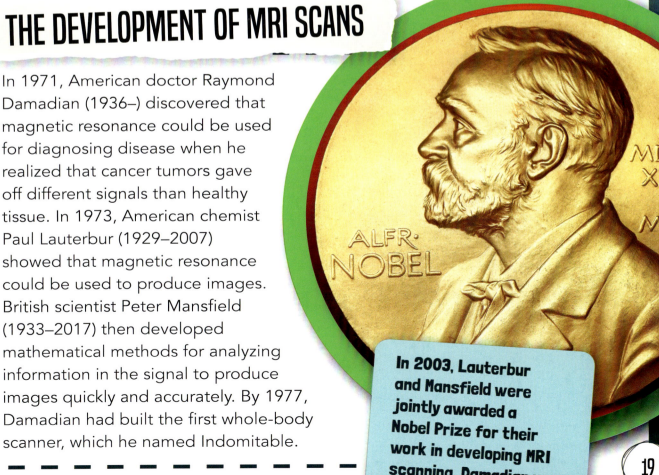

In 2003, Lauterbur and Mansfield were jointly awarded a Nobel Prize for their work in developing MRI scanning. Damadian was

ULTRASOUND SCANS

An ultrasound scan, or sonogram, uses high-frequency sound waves to produce an image of part of the inside of a patient's body. The technology involved is similar to the **ECHOLOCATION** used by bats, dolphins, and whales. A small, handheld instrument, called a transducer probe, is used to give off the high-frequency sound waves. It also picks up the waves as they are echoed back by the part of the body being scanned. Ultrasound scans usually take between 15 and 45 minutes and are generally carried out in a hospital by a specially trained health-care professional called a sonographer.

Transducer probes come in all shapes and sizes.

Gel is applied so that the probe moves easily and there is contact at all times between the probe and the skin.

DIFFERENT TYPES OF ULTRASOUND SCAN

There are three main types of ultrasound scan:
- External, in which the probe is moved over the skin
- Internal, in which the probe is inserted into the body to look at organs such as the **UTERUS**
- Endoscopy, in which the probe is attached to a thin flexible tube that can be passed further into the body to look at areas such as the stomach

USES OF ULTRASOUND SCANS

Ultrasound scans are commonly used to examine pregnant women. They are used to check the developing baby in the uterus and to work out when the baby will be born. They can also be used to try to find out whether the baby is a boy or a girl, or if the mother is carrying more than one baby. They can also be used to see the inside of a patient's heart and to measure the flow of blood through the heart and the main blood vessels. Ultrasound scans are also used to examine joints and muscles and to detect cancer in the kidneys, liver, and other organs. In an emergency, for example if a patient has been involved in a car accident, doctors need to diagnose problems such as internal bleeding very quickly and ultrasound scans can be a useful tool. Ultrasound can also be used to guide a biopsy (see page 7), so that tissue is removed from exactly the right spot. Ultrasound machines can also produce 3-D images that are particularly useful for diagnosing cancers and for checking the development of unborn babies.

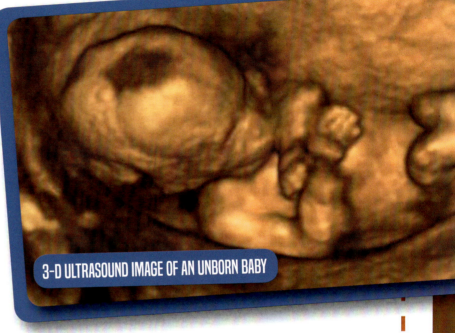
3-D ULTRASOUND IMAGE OF AN UNBORN BABY

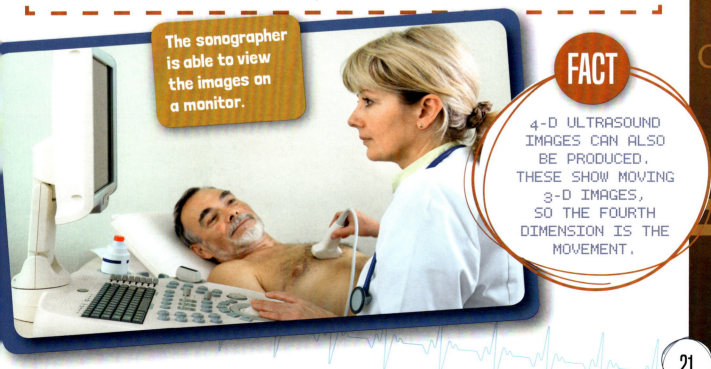
The sonographer is able to view the images on a monitor.

FACT

4-D ULTRASOUND IMAGES CAN ALSO BE PRODUCED. THESE SHOW MOVING 3-D IMAGES, SO THE FOURTH DIMENSION IS THE MOVEMENT.

HOW DO ULTRASOUND SCANS WORK?

The ultrasound machine sends high-frequency sound wave pulses into the patient's body, using the probe. Wave frequency is measured in hertz (Hz) and refers to the number of waves that pass a given point in one second. The frequency of ultrasound waves is above 20,000 Hz.

0 Hz — 16 — 20 000
Infrasound | Audible frequencies | Ultrasound

Ultrasound waves have a very high frequency that cannot be heard by the human ear.

As they travel into the body, the ultrasound waves hit boundaries, for example between bone and muscle. Some of the sound waves are reflected back to the probe, rather like echoes. Some travel farther before being reflected back. The reflected waves that the probe picks up are passed back to a central processing unit (CPU). The CPU calculates the distance from the probe to the various body tissues and organs and the time of each echo's return. It uses this information to create an image that is displayed on a monitor.

FACT

MILLIONS OF SOUND WAVE PULSES AND RETURNING ECHOES ARE SENT AND RECEIVED EVERY SECOND.

The transducer probe acts as both the mouth and ears of the ultrasound machine, sending out and receiving sound waves.

THE DISCOVERY AND DEVELOPMENT OF ULTRASOUND

In 1880, two French physicists, Pierre Curie (1859–1906) and Paul-Jacques Curie (1855–1941), discovered the **PIEZOELECTRIC EFFECT**. Inside a scanner probe are piezoelectric crystals that send out and receive sound waves. When an electric current is applied, they change shape rapidly and produce sound waves. When returning sound waves hit the crystals, they emit electrical currents. The CPU uses this data to produce images.

Following the 1912 sinking of the *Titanic*, French physicist Paul Langevin (1872–1946) invented the first transducer in 1915 to detect objects on the seabed.

In 1942, Karl Dussik was the first to use ultrasound for medical purposes, diagnosing a brain tumor in a patient. In the 1950s, other ultrasound equipment was developed to detect breast cancer. In 1958, Dr. Ian Donald became the first to use ultrasound to examine pregnant women. In 1966, an ultrasound technology called Doppler was invented that showed blood flow through the heart. Color Doppler images followed in the 1970s. In the 1980s, 3-D ultrasound technology was invented by Kazunori Baba in Japan. In the 1990s, ultrasound became commonplace and 4-D images became available.

Doppler ultrasound scans are also often used to test for deep vein thrombosis (DVT), a condition in which blood clots form in veins.

PET SCANS

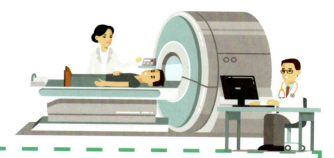

Positron Emission Tomography (PET) scans are used to provide detailed 3-D images of the inside of the body. Rather than just showing how a body part looks, PET scans also provide information about how well that body part is working. PET scans show what is happening in the cells of the body. This is very important because some diseases cause changes in the body's cells that cannot be picked up by other types of imaging such as MRI or CT scans. PET scans are sometimes combined with MRI or CT scans to produce even more detailed images.

A COMBINED PET-CT SCANNER

PET scans can be used to:
- Detect cancer
- Find out how big a tumor is, if the cancer has spread, and how well any treatment is working
- Detect heart disease
- Diagnose brain conditions
- Plan delicate operations such as brain surgery for **EPILEPSY**

HOW DO PET SCANS WORK?

Patients who are having a PET scan are first injected with a **RADIOACTIVE** substance called a radiotracer (also called a tracer). The tracer gives off radiation in the form of gamma rays. (Look back to page 8 to remind yourself about the electromagnetic spectrum.) The tracer that is often used is called fluorodeoxyglucose (FDG). FDG is very similar to a naturally occurring substance called glucose (a type of sugar) that the body uses to make energy. The PET scanner contains a gamma camera that picks up the radiation that is given off by the tracer and looks at areas where the tracer builds up. It then uses this information to work out if there are any abnormal tissues and also how well the body part being scanned is working. A buildup of FDG can highlight cancer, for example, because cancer cells use up glucose much more quickly than healthy cells.

A PET scanner looks like a giant letter "O."

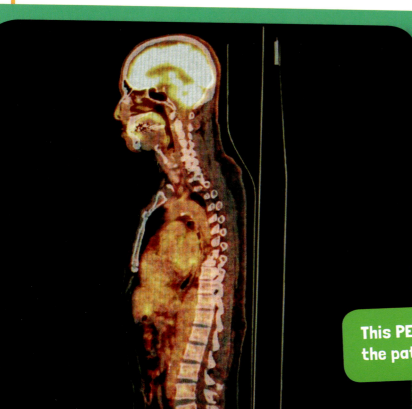

This PET scan is showing the patient's spine.

HAVING A PET SCAN

The radiotracer is usually injected into a vein in the patient's arm. Sometimes it is given as a drink or in the form of a gas that the patient inhales. It takes about an hour for it to get into the cells of the body. Moving around and speaking affect how the tracer moves through the body, so during this time the patient needs to keep still and quiet. The patient then lies on a moveable bed that slides into the center of the ring-shaped scanner. Patients who feel anxious in the enclosed space of the scanner may be given a sedative to help them to relax. As this type of scan involves the use of radiation, the radiographer sits in the next room, where the monitoring equipment is housed. A PET scan is painless and usually takes between 30 and 45 minutes. The patient has to remain completely still and quiet throughout. After the scan, the tracer quickly loses its radioactivity. Drinking lots of water helps to flush it out of the body.

The radiographer can see the patient throughout and the patient has a buzzer to press in case of any problems.

FACT SINCE PET SCANS USE RADIATION, THERE IS A VERY SMALL RISK OF TISSUE DAMAGE. BUT THE AMOUNT OF RADIATION IS ONLY ABOUT THE SAME AS THAT FROM NATURAL SOURCES, LIKE THE SUN, OVER A THREE-YEAR PERIOD.

Modern PET scanners gradually evolved thanks to numerous scientific discoveries. In 1932, Carl Anderson, an American physicist, discovered positrons – tiny particles with a positive charge. In 1949, Benedictine Cassen developed the scintillation (say: sihn-tih-LAY-shun) scanner, a device that could detect radioactivity. In 1952, David Kuhl developed a better version called the photoscanner. During the 1950s, another American physicist, Gordon Brownell, and an American doctor, William Sweet, developed positron scanning equipment that detected a brain tumor in a seven-year-old girl. This technology led to the invention of the first PET scanner during the 1970s by Edward Hoffman, Michel Ter-Pogossian, and Michael Phelps.

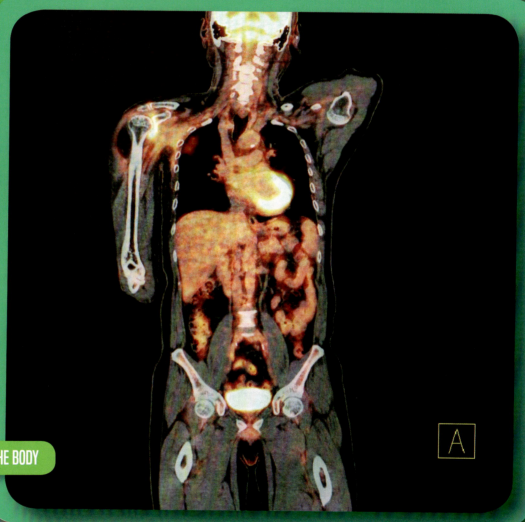

A PET SCAN OF THE BODY

Since then, the quality of PET scan images has slowly improved, thanks to advances like better computer programs and radiation sensors. Modern PET scanners are very expensive and only a few hundred are in use around the world.

PET scan images are now incredibly detailed.

SCANS IN THE FUTURE

TELEMEDICINE

Research is continuing into the effective use of portable ultrasound equipment. This equipment can send information in real time to experts in other places or hospitals, even in other parts of the world. Using a smartphone or other smart device, the expert is able to guide and instruct the person carrying out the ultrasound scan. The expert can then immediately look at the results and plan treatment for the patient. This type of care is an example of telemedicine – using telecommunications to provide patient care. It can provide rapid, lifesaving care in emergency situations, such as war zones, natural disasters, and road traffic accidents. It is also useful in less economically developed countries (LEDCs), where medical experts may not be available. This type of care also means that the patient may not have to be moved to a hospital and that no time is lost in starting lifesaving treatment.

Telemedicine can link patients in remote or dangerous places with medical experts.

THE FUTURE OF PET SCANNING

Research is also continuing into ways to produce cheaper PET scanners, so that they are available to more of the world's people, whether they live in economically developed countries or less-developed countries. At present, PET scanners are most commonly found in the U.S., parts of Europe, Japan, and Australia. In the future, it may be possible to combine PET, MRI, and CT scans into a single examination. This would enable even earlier and more accurate diagnosis of diseases. Work is also continuing into the development of different radiotracers that could be used to seek out specific types of cancer in the body.

NANOPARTICLES

Nanoparticles are unbelievably tiny particles of matter. They occur naturally in substances like ash and dust. Fires, engines, and mining also produce nanoparticles. They are also found in some health-care products and cosmetics such as sunscreen. Some nanoparticles may cause health problems. By "labeling" nanoparticles with long-lasting radiotracers, it might be possible to use PET scanning to find out how nanoparticles move around in the human body.

Researchers are working to produce nanoparticles that can be used to deliver cancer drugs directly to the affected cells.

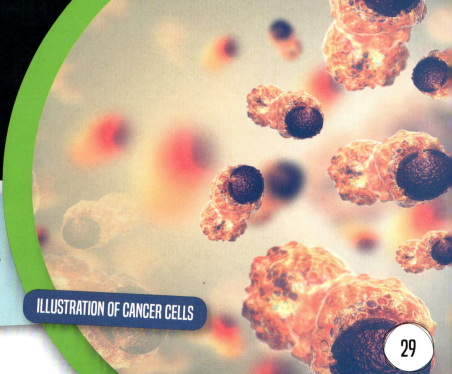

ILLUSTRATION OF CANCER CELLS

DEXA SCANS

DEXA SCANNER

DEXA scans are used to measure the density of a patient's bones and to diagnose a disease called osteoporosis. This is a condition in which the bones lose tissue and become weak and likely to break. DEXA scanning equipment aims two X-ray beams with different energy levels at the patient's bones, usually the hip and spine. One type is absorbed by soft tissue and the other is absorbed by bone. Special detectors in the DEXA scanner measure how much radiation passes through the bones. The more dense the bone is, the fewer X-rays pass through to the detectors. These measurements are then compared with those of other people of the same sex and **ETHNICITY** and of a similar age and weight. If a patient is found to be suffering from osteoporosis or is thought to be likely to develop it, they can be given medication to strengthen the bones.

During the scan, the scanning arm is passed over the patient's body.

FACT

DEXA STANDS FOR DUAL-ENERGY X-RAY ABSORPTIOMETRY. DEXA SCANS ARE ALSO CALLED BONE MINERAL DENSITY SCANS.

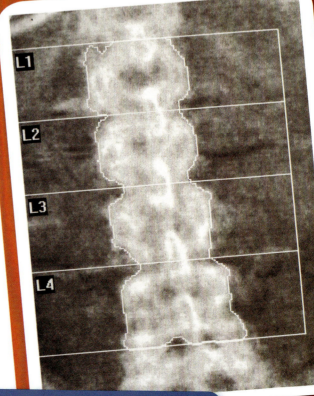

DEXA SPINE SCAN SHOWING OSTEOPOROSIS

GLOSSARY

ALZHEIMER'S DISEASE a brain disease, usually affecting older people, that causes memory loss

ATOM the basic unit making up a chemical element such as oxygen or hydrogen

CANCER a serious disease caused by abnormal body cells dividing out of control

CARTILAGE firm, flexible connective tissue found in various parts of the body including joints

CELLS the basic building blocks of all living things

CLAUSTROPHOBIC frightened of enclosed spaces

CREST the highest point

CROSS-SECTIONAL shown by making a straight cut across a solid form

CYSTIC FIBROSIS a disease that causes a buildup of thick, sticky mucus in the lungs and other organs

ECHOLOCATION the location of objects using reflected sound waves

ELECTRODES electrical conductors that carry electricity

EPILEPSY a brain condition that causes seizures (bursts of electrical activity in the brain that temporarily affect how it works)

ETHNICITY a person's national or cultural identity

EXPLORATORY SURGERY an operation carried out to find out what is causing a patient's symptoms

GENERAL ANESTHETIC a medical substance given to a patient that causes loss of consciousness

HEALTH-CARE PROFESSIONALS doctors, nurses, and other trained specialists who provide treatment for patients

HIGH-VOLTAGE describing high-powered electrical energy at a voltage over 600 volts

HYDROGEN a colorless, odorless gas that, on Earth, occurs mainly combined with oxygen as water

LIGAMENT tough, flexible tissue that connects bones or holds a joint together

MAGNETIC FIELDS the areas around magnets where there is a magnetic force

MICROSCOPE a piece of scientific equipment that makes things look many times bigger

MOLECULE a group of atoms bonded together

MULTIPLE SCLEROSIS a condition affecting the brain and/or spinal cord that can cause vision, movement, and balance problems

NOBEL PRIZE a set of six international annual awards, established in the will of Swedish scientist Alfred Nobel and given to recognize advances made in fields such as science and medicine

ORGANS parts of an organism with specific, important functions, for example the brain and lungs

OXYGEN a colorless gas found in the atmosphere

PACEMAKERS man-made medical devices for regulating the heartbeat

PHOSPHORUS a poisonous chemical element, one form of which is used in making matches

PHOTOGRAPHIC PLATE one of the earliest forms of photographic film

PIEZOELECTRIC EFFECT the ability of some materials to produce electricity when pressure is applied to them

RADIOACTIVE giving off radiation

RADIO WAVES a type of electromagnetic radiation

RESEARCH investigations and experiments carried out to discover new information

SCREEN test for the presence or absence of a disease

SYMPTOMS indicators, for example pain, that a patient is suffering from a particular disease or condition

THREE-DIMENSIONAL having or showing length, width, and depth

TUMOR a swelling caused by abnormal growth of body tissue

TWO-DIMENSIONAL having or showing length and width but no depth

UTERUS the organ in the female body in which offspring develop

INDEX

A
Alzheimer's disease 19
atoms 17

B
Baba, Kazunori 23
babies 5, 15, 18, 21, 18
Brownell, Gordon 27

C
cancer 7, 10, 14–16, 19, 21, 23–26, 29
cells 17, 24–26, 29
central processing units (CPUs) 22–23
children 6, 14, 16
contrast agents 10, 13
Cormack, Allan McLeod 15
CT scans 12–16, 24, 29
Curie, Paul-Jacques 23
Curie, Pierre 23
cystic fibrosis 10, 14

D
Damadian, Raymond 19
dentists 10
DEXA scans 30
Donald, Ian 23
Dussik, Karl 23

E
echolocation 20
electromagnetic radiation 8
electromagnetic spectrum 8, 25
endoscopy 20
epilepsy 24

G
gamma rays 8, 25

H
Hoffman, Edward 27
Hounsfield, Godfrey 15
hydrogen 17

I
images
- cross-sectional 13
- four-dimensional 21
- three-dimensional 12–13, 21, 24
- two-dimensional 12–13
imaging 6, 15–16, 24

K
Kuhl, David 27

L
Langevin, Paul 23
Lauterbur, Paul 19

M
magnetic fields 16–18
mammography 7
Mansfield, Peter 19
molecules 17
MRI scans 6, 16–19, 24, 29

O
organs 14, 16, 20–22
oxygen 11, 17

P
PET scans 24–27, 29
piezoelectric effect 23
protons 17

R
radiation 8–9, 11, 13, 15–16, 25–27, 30
radiographers 12, 14, 16–18, 26
radiologists 6
radiology 6
radiotracers 25–26, 29
radio waves 8, 16–17
research 15, 28–29
Röntgen, Anna Bertha 11
Röntgen, Wilhelm 11

S
scanners 6, 13, 14–19, 23, 24–27, 29–30
screening 7
sonographers 20–21
strokes 14, 16, 19
Sweet, William 27

T
Ter-Pogossian, Michel 27
transducer probes 20, 22

U
ultrasound 20–23, 28

W
water 17, 19, 26
wavelengths 8
wave frequencies 22

X
X-rays 4, 6, 8–13, 15–16, 30